P9-DGB-619

Red Pandas

Laura Marsh

NATIONAL
GEOGRAPHIC

Washington, D.C.

For Shelby —L. F. M.

Copyright © 2015 National Geographic Society

Published by National Geographic Partners, LLC, Washington, D.C. 20036.

All rights reserved. Reproduction in whole or in part without written permission of the publisher is prohibited.

Trade paperback ISBN: 978-1-4263-2121-4
Reinforced library binding ISBN: 978-1-4263-2122-1

Editor: Shelby Alinsky
Art Director: Amanda Larsen
Editorial: Snapdragon Books
Designer: YAY! Design
Photo Editor: Lori Epstein
Production Assistants: Sanjida Rashid and Rachel Kenny
Rights Clearance Specialist: Colm McKeveny
Manufacturing Manager: Rachel Faulise

The author and publisher gratefully acknowledge the expert content review of this book by Brian Williams of the Red Panda Network and the literacy review of this book by Mariam Jean Dreher, professor of reading education at the University of Maryland, College Park. Find out how to become a Red Panda Ranger at redpandanetwork.org.

Illustration Credits
Cover, Shin Yoshino/Minden Pictures; 1, Juan Carlos Munoz/Nature Picture Library; 3, Eric Isselée/iStockphoto; 5, Frans Lanting/National Geographic Creative; 6, inga spence/Alamy; 7, Juniors Bildarchiv GmbH/Alamy; 9, Aaron Ferster/Photo Researchers RM/Getty Images; 10–11, blickwinkel/Alamy; 12, Krys Bailey/Alamy; 13, Katherine Feng/Minden Pictures; 14–15, Gary Randall Photography/Kimball Stock; 15, Juan Carlos Munoz/Nature Picture Library; 16 (UP), Juniors Bildarchiv GmbH/Alamy; 16 (LO), Paulina Lenting-Smulders/E+/Getty Images; 17 (UP), Jennifer Diehl/Fort Wayne Children's Zoo; 17 (CTR), A & J Visage/Alamy; 17 (LO), imageBROKER/Alamy; 18–19, Dr. Axel Gebauer/NPL/Minden Pictures; 20, Dr. Axel Gebauer/NPL/Minden Pictures; 21 (UP), WILDLIFE GmbH/Alamy; 21 (CTR), WILDLIFE GmbH/Alamy; 21 (LO), WILDLIFE GmbH/Alamy; 22, JGA/Shutterstock; 24–25, Staffan Widstrand/Nature Picture Library; 26, Dr. Axel Gebauer/Nature Picture Library; 27, Chris Scharf, Red Panda Network Ambassador; 28, Chris Scharf, Red Panda Network Ambassador; 28 (INSET), csp_sophie_tea/Fotosearch; 29, Cyril Hou/Alamy; 30 (LE), Jak Wonderly; 30 (RT), Bambax/Shutterstock; 31 (UPLE), ang intaravichian/Shutterstock; 31 (UPRT), Jak Wonderly; 31 (LOLE), Bildagentur Zoonar GmbH/Shutterstock; 31 (LORT), JGA/Shutterstock; 32 (UPLE), Jak Wonderly; 32 (UPRT), Karine Aigner/National Geographic Creative; 32 (LOLE), Chris Godfrey Wildlife Photography/Alamy; 32 (LORT), Andy Poole/Shutterstock; header (THROUGHOUT), ang intaravichian/Shutterstock; vocab (THROUGHOUT), Leremy/Shutterstock

National Geographic supports K–12 educators with ELA Common Core Resources.
Visit natgeoed.org/commoncore for more information.

Printed in the United States of America
16/WOR/3

Table of Contents

Guess Who? 4

A Forest Home 8

Life in the Trees 10

Lots of Leaves 12

Day Sleeper 14

5 Fun Facts About Red Pandas 16

Little Ones 18

Something to Say 22

Home Area 24

Hide-and-Seek 26

What in the World? 30

Glossary 32

Guess Who?

It's the size of a cat.
But it's not that.

It has ears like a bear.
But it's much more rare.

It's out with the moon.
But it's not a raccoon.

Do you need another clue?
Or can you guess who?

It's a red panda!

Many people know about giant pandas. They are big and have black and white fur.

Giant panda

Q What is red and white and goes round and round?

A A red panda stuck in a revolving door!

Red pandas share the name "panda." But red pandas and giant pandas are different animals.

A red panda is sometimes called a firefox. Yet a fox and a red panda are not in the same family, either.

Red panda

7

A Forest Home

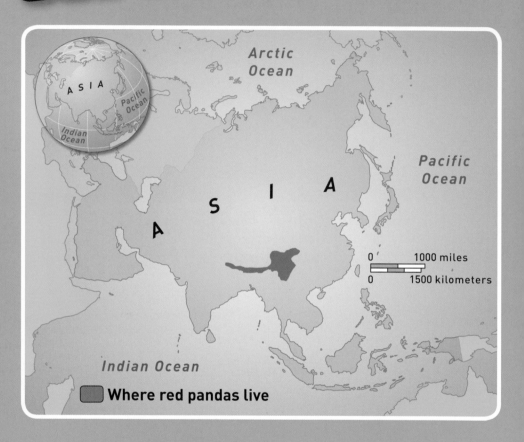

Arctic Ocean

ASIA

Pacific Ocean

Indian Ocean

A S I A

A

Pacific Ocean

0   1000 miles
0   1500 kilometers

Indian Ocean

Where red pandas live

Red pandas live in mountain forests in Asia. It gets cold in the mountains.

So red pandas have thick fur all over. Even the bottoms of their feet have fur. All of this fur keeps them warm.

Life in the Trees

Red pandas are super climbers! They run quickly over branches. A red panda's body helps it live in the trees.

TAIL: A long tail helps it balance on tree branches.

FEET: Fur on the bottoms of its feet keeps it from slipping on wet tree branches.

WRIST BONE: This long bone acts like a thumb. It helps a red panda hang on to branches.

CLAWS: Sharp claws grip the trees while it climbs.

Panda Words

BALANCE: to stay up and not fall over

GRIP: to hold on tightly

Lots of Leaves

Red pandas find food in trees and on the ground. They eat lots and lots of bamboo leaves. They also munch on fruit, grass, and mushrooms.

Bamboo leaves are a favorite food.

Day Sleeper

Red pandas dangle their legs when it's hot.

Red pandas are active early in the morning and at sunset. They are often active at night, too. But they rest in the middle of the day.

Panda Word

ACTIVE: likely to move around a lot

They curl up when it's cold.

5 FUN FACTS
About Red Pandas

1

Red pandas have very long tails. Their tails are almost as long as their bodies.

They lick themselves clean, like a house cat does. This is called grooming.

2

Newborns have hardly any fur on the bottoms of their feet. The fur grows as they get older.

3

4

In winter, they may spend up to 13 hours a day looking for bamboo and eating it.

5

Red pandas eat about 200,000 bamboo leaves every day.

Little Ones

A mother makes a nest out of sticks, leaves, and grass. She will have her babies in the nest.

Between one and four babies will be born. They are called cubs.

A red panda nest is usually in a tree.

19

Cubs don't look red when they are born. They are grayish brown. They drink milk and grow bigger. Then their fur turns red.

The mother moves her cub by picking it up in her mouth.

Something to Say

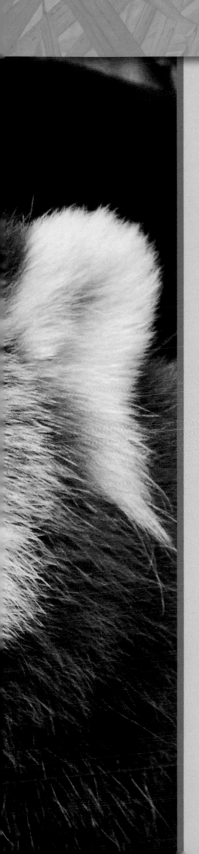

When cubs make a high whistle (WISS-ul), their mom comes running. It means the cubs need something— right now!

Adult red pandas also make noises. They may twitter, squeak, or snort.

Home Area

Red pandas mostly live alone. Each red panda lives in its own area it calls home.

Sometimes another red panda stops by. But it won't stay for long.

Hide-and-Seek

Can you find the red panda?

Red pandas are shy.
They hide when a predator
(PRED-uh-ter) is near.
They blend in with the forest.
Their black fur matches the
shadows. Their red fur
matches
moss on
the trees.

Panda Word

PREDATOR: an animal
that hunts and
eats other animals

Red moss on the trees

We are still learning about red pandas. They are hard to find and study in the wild.

People are trying to save the forests where red pandas live. If we save the forests, we can save their homes.

What in the World?

These pictures are up-close views of things in a red panda's world. Use the hints to figure out what's in the pictures. Answers are on page 31.

1

HINT: This part is striped like a raccoon.

2

HINT: Red pandas spend a lot of time here.

Word Bank

nest   claws   tail   leaves   trees   fur

3

HINT: They eat a lot of these.

4

HINT: Red pandas have this all over.

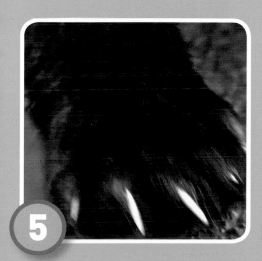

5

HINT: These are used for climbing.

6

HINT: Cubs live here after they are born.

Answers: 1. tail, 2. trees, 3. leaves, 4. fur, 5. claws, 6. nest

ACTIVE: likely to move
around a lot

BALANCE: to stay up
and not fall over

GRIP: to hold on tightly

PREDATOR: an animal that
hunts and eats other animals